MAPPING RIVERS

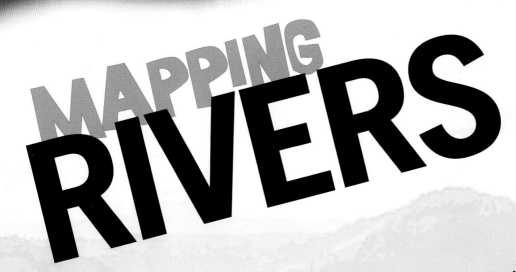

Louise Spilsbury

www.heinemann.co.uk/library
Visit our website to find out more information about Heinemann Library books.

To order:
☎ Phone 44 (0) 1865 888066
▤ Send a fax to 44 (0) 1865 314091
▭ Visit the Heinemann Bookshop at www.heinemann.co.uk/library to browse our catalogue and order online.

First published in Great Britain by Heinemann Library, Halley Court, Jordan Hill, Oxford OX2 8EJ, part of Harcourt Education.
Heinemann is a registered trademark of Harcourt Education Ltd.

© Harcourt Education Ltd 2005

Editorial: Lucy Thunder and Harriet Milles
Design: Ron Kamen and Celia Jones
Illustrations: Barry Atkinson, Darren Lingard and Jeff Edwards
Picture Research: Melissa Allison and Beatrice Ray
Production: Camilla Smith

Originated by Repro Multi Warna
Printed and bound in China by WKT Company Limited

The paper used to print this book comes from sustainable resources.

10 dig ISBN 0 431 01322 5 (hardback)
13 dig ISBN 978 0 431 01322 0
09 08 07 06
10 9 8 7 6 5 4 3 2 1

10 dig ISBN 0 431 013276 (paperback)
13 dig ISBN 978 0 431 01327 5
09 08 07 06
10 9 8 7 6 5 4 3 2 1

British Library Cataloguing in Publication Data

Spilsbury, Louise
  (Mapping the UK). – Mapping Rivers
  526'.091693

A full catalogue record for this book is available from the British Library.

Acknowledgements

The Publishers would like to thank the following for permission to reproduce photographs:
Alamy Images pp. 8, 16, 23; Corbis Royalty-free pp. 5, 12 (marsh, lake, woodland); Corbis/Jason Hawkes p. 7b; GetMapping p. 18; Getty Images/Photodisc pp. 12 (slope, road), 24 (Mississippi, globe), 25 (Danube, Yantze); Harcourt Education Ltd/ Peter Evans pp. 6, 11b, 12 (river, stream), 20, 25 (Nile), 26; istockphoto.com p. 24 (Amazon); Jane Hance p. 12 (campsite); London Aerial Photo Library p. 10; Oxford Scientific Films p. 7t; Philips Maps p. 21b; Photomap p. 11t; Reproduced by permission of Ordnance Survey on behalf of The Controller of Her Majesty's Stationery Office, © Crown Copyright 100000230 pp. 15, 19, 21t; Skyscan p. 12 (canal); Skyscan Photolibrary p. 23.

Cover photograph of the River Wye at Symonds Yat, Herefordshire, reproduced with permission of Harcourt Education Ltd/Peter Evans. Section of Ordnance Survey map reproduced by permission of Ordnance Survey on behalf of The Controller of Her Majesty's Stationery Office, © Crown Copyright 100000230.

The Publishers would like to thank Margaret Mackintosh, Honorary Editor of Primary Geographer, for her assistance in the preparation of this book.

Every effort has been made to contact copyright holders of any material reproduced in this book. Any omissions will be rectified in subsequent printings if notice is given to the Publishers.

Disclaimer

Contents

Words appearing in the text in bold, **like this**, are explained in the Glossary.

▶ Look out for this symbol! When you see it next to a question, you will find the answer on page 29.

What are maps?

Have you ever been lost in a shopping centre or a fun park? Perhaps you looked at a map to find out where you were? A map is a drawing of a place that helps us to find out where things are. There are many different kinds of maps. You can have a map of a small place, like a school, or a map of a huge area, like a country.

A bird's-eye view

Maps are **aerial** views of places. That means they show places from above. Imagine you are flying in a helicopter, looking down on the land below. You are getting an aerial view of an area. We usually look at things from the side, or at an angle, but things look really different when seen from above. Try looking around at the things in your room. Then put some of them on the floor and look straight down on them from above. This will help you to start seeing the world as maps do!

Hi there! I'm Carta. Are you ready for the journey of a lifetime? Stick with me as we explore rivers, and together we'll find out just how useful and how much fun maps can be!

This is a simple map of a house by a river, based on the picture on the left.

Keeping it real

Another important fact you need to know about maps is that they only show **permanent features**. A map of a river will not show boats on the water – only the things that are there all the time. Mapmakers have to choose what to put in and what to leave out. They do this because you can't show every detail about a place on a single piece of paper.

A mapping adventure

In this book you will find out how rivers form, what special features they have, and how these features are shown on different kinds of maps. On some of the maps you will notice we have put coloured 'spotlights' over places or features. These are to help you find things more easily.

Always remember to stay safe when you are by a river. Keep to the banks and stay well away from fast flowing water.

Looking at rivers

All rivers are different but most have been formed in a similar way. So let's take a trip down a typical river to find out how rivers work. Remember, water flows downhill!

The upper course

The place where a river starts is called its **source**. A river's source might be a **spring**, a lake, or a stream filled by rainfall. A source is usually on high ground – on a mountain or a hill. As water from the source flows downhill, other streams and rivers join it, and the river gets bigger. It carves a deep groove called a **valley** through the rocky landscape.

Rivers fill up because of the water cycle. Heat from the Sun **evaporates** water from lakes and seas. When the air cools down, the water falls from the sky as rain and snow. It drains from the land into streams and rivers.

The water in the upper course of a river swirls about wildly over rocks. It often passes over **waterfalls** and **rapids**.

This is the middle course of a river. The bends in the river are called meanders.

The middle course

As the river reaches lower ground where the land is less steep, it has less energy. The water flows in a **channel**. This becomes wider in the river's middle course. The river starts to wind and form large bends, called **meanders**, often around areas of harder rock.

The lower course

Just as you slow down when you reach the bottom of a slide, water flows more gently over flat land in its lower course. The channel is usually at its widest point here, and contains most water. The place where a river opens wide as it flows into the sea is called its **mouth**. Some mouths widen out into **estuaries**. Many rivers flow into the sea like this, but some flow into lakes or even into other rivers.

The lower part of a river is wide. This is because the channel has broadened out as other rivers and streams have joined it along the way.

7

Marking rivers on a map

Have you ever tried to draw a map? It is hard to imagine how a place really looks from above, isn't it? Mapmakers use **aerial** photographs taken by cameras in aeroplanes or **satellites** to help them make maps.

Looking at an aerial photo

The aerial photo on this page shows the **mouth** of the River Seiont in Wales. In the upper course of a river, rough water breaks off mud and rocks from the **riverbed** and **banks**. This is called **erosion**. These bits are carried along with the water. When the river reaches flatter land near the sea, it has less energy and flows gently. The bits of eroded rock and mud have been ground up into small bits by the water. Now they are **deposited** at the sides or on the bed of the river to form mudflats.

This is an aerial view of the River Seiont in Wales. Can you see the mudflats in this photograph?

Making a map

The sketch map below is drawn from the aerial photograph on the page opposite. This map uses colours and shapes to show what things are. The blue area is the river. The brown area is the mud, or **sediment**, deposited on the banks from upstream. The green area is fields and the patches of darker green are woodland. The area of buildings is shown in pink and the major roads and the car parks are shown in grey.

Why don't you try to draw a simple sketch map like the one below from a different aerial view? Perhaps you could use a photo from a magazine, or find one of a place near your home.

This sketch map is drawn from the photograph on page 8.

Along the River Thames

Let's take a look at a real river – the Thames. While some rivers in the UK start on high ground, the landscape in the south and east of England is generally flatter. Here many rivers, including the River Thames, flow on lowish, gently sloping land. The Thames flows and **meanders** slowly all the way from its **source** to the sea.

London and the Thames

The Thames flows through London. London became the capital city of England because the river formed an important trade route between England and the rest of the world. Goods such as tea, spices, and fruit from abroad were unloaded there from cargo ships. These days, cargo ships are too big to unload at London. Most of the boats on the Thames are taking tourists on sightseeing trips.

> ► What are the names of the three green bridges over the Thames in the picture on the right? (You can find out by looking at the labels on the photomap!)

This is an **aerial** photograph of the River Thames. Can you see the meanders it makes through London?

This map is called a photomap. It uses an aerial photograph of London, but the roads have been coloured in and street names have been added.

This big wheel is called the London Eye. Can you find it on the photomap above? The important-looking buildings on the right river **bank** are the Houses of Parliament.

River symbols

If you draw a map, you may write labels on things, such as rivers, roads, and churches, to show what they are. That is fine, but most maps would get too cluttered if everything on them were labelled! This is why most maps use colours and symbols to represent things.

Simply symbols

Symbols are simple pictures, shapes, lines, or even letters that represent real things. We use symbols all the time. When you draw a smiley face to show you are happy, you are using a symbol! On a real map you will see lots of symbols around river areas. Some represent natural features, such as marshes. Others show features that people have built, such as bridges.

Lots of settlements are built around rivers. Place names can tell us where on a river a place is. ▶ If Cambridge is a town built around a bridge on the River Cam, where do you think Dartmouth is?

These are some of the features found around rivers. Beside the photos are the symbols used to represent them on maps. When you make maps, try making up some of your own symbols.

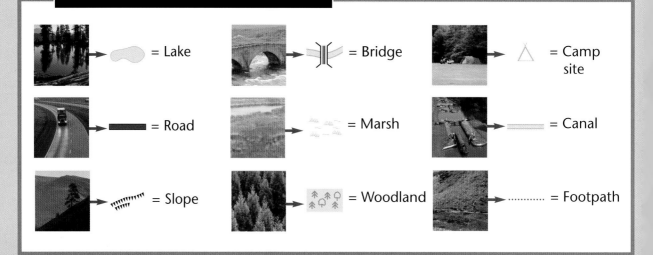

= Lake

= Bridge

= Camp site

= Road

= Marsh

= Canal

= Slope

= Woodland

= Footpath

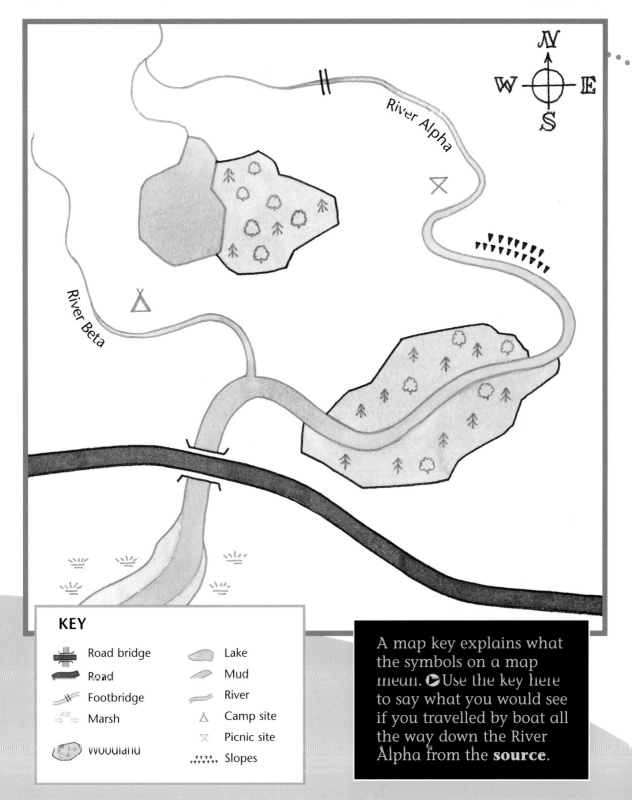

KEY

	Road bridge		Lake
	Road		Mud
	Footbridge		River
	Marsh	△	Camp site
	Woodland	⋈	Picnic site
			Slopes

A map key explains what the symbols on a map mean. ◖Use the key here to say what you would see if you travelled by boat all the way down the River Alpha from the **source**.

Map detectives

Map symbols can give you lots of clues about how people use rivers. For instance, people travel across rivers by bridges. **Reservoirs** store river water to be carried to taps in homes. Tourists visit camp sites near rivers, to go fishing, boating, or swimming. Farms use river water for crops and for animals to drink.

Locating rivers

One way to find things on a map is to use compass directions – north, east, south, and west. Most maps are drawn with north at the top, so you can describe where something is by giving its direction from something else. In the sketch map below, the lake is north of the road and west of the woods.

Getting to grips with grids

Have you noticed the rows of squares that form a grid over real maps? Grids help you to find exactly where things are. In the sketch map below, the lines going up (vertically) have letters. The lines going across (horizontally) have numbers. You can describe where something is by giving its grid reference. For example, on this map the lake is in square B,4. (Go to page 28 to find more help with reading grid references.)

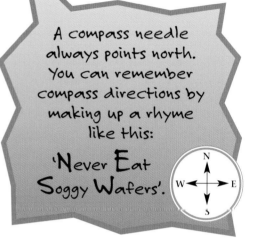

A compass needle always points north. You can remember compass directions by making up a rhyme like this:

'Never Eat Soggy Wafers'.

Confluence is the word for the point where a stream or river flows into another river. ▷ What is the grid reference for the confluence of the Alpha and Beta rivers in this map?

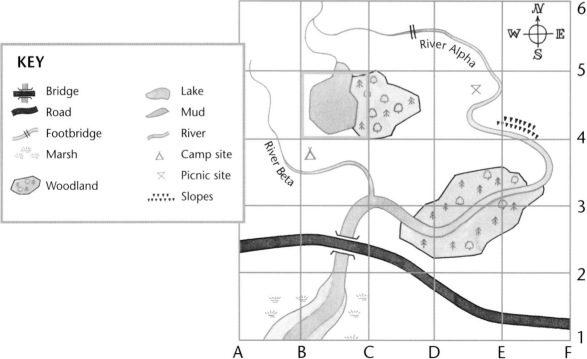

KEY

⊞	Bridge	🍃	Lake
▬	Road	🍂	Mud
⫫	Footbridge	〰	River
⁖⁖	Marsh	△	Camp site
🌲	Woodland	✕	Picnic site
		ˌˌˌˌ	Slopes

Grid games

The map on this page is a small section of an **Ordnance Survey** map. It shows part of the River Severn flowing through Upton upon Severn in Worcestershire. Large maps like this have numbers for both the vertical and the horizontal lines. To read a grid reference, we give the number on the vertical line first and then the number on the horizontal line. (Remember this by the phrase: 'Along the corridor and up the stairs'.) So, the grid reference for the Marina is 85, 40 and for Merevale Farm it is 83, 42.

▶ Can you solve these map puzzles? What is the name of the castle in 84, 42? What is the grid reference for the bridge across the river at Upton upon Severn? What is the name of the village in 87, 39?

The ups and downs of rivers

Near its **source** on high ground, a river flows down steep slopes. Fast-moving water has a lot of energy. In its upper course, a river carves narrow, steep-sided **valleys** into the land. As a river flows downhill, it passes over land that becomes less and less steep. Here, the water flows more gently, creating **channels** that are wider and shallower. How do maps show all these slopes?

Contour lines

When you look at river valleys on maps, their slopes are most likely to be shown by pale brown lines called contour lines. Mapmakers draw contour lines to join up areas of land that are the same height above sea level. The diagrams on the opposite page show you how contour lines work.

Contour lines are tricky to understand! The important thing to remember is that when they are close together it means a slope is steep. When contour lines are far apart, the slopes are gentler and the land is flatter.

This is a river flowing through the bottom of a steep-sided valley.

a) A river valley

b) Here you can see how mapmakers draw contour lines on a slope. Contour lines join up land that is the same height above sea level. In this picture the contour lines are drawn at every 10 metres above sea level.

c) On a map, the contour lines of a valley look like this. You are looking down from above. The numbers on the lines show how many metres above sea level the land measures at certain places on the slope. The lines that are closer together show where the slope gets steeper.

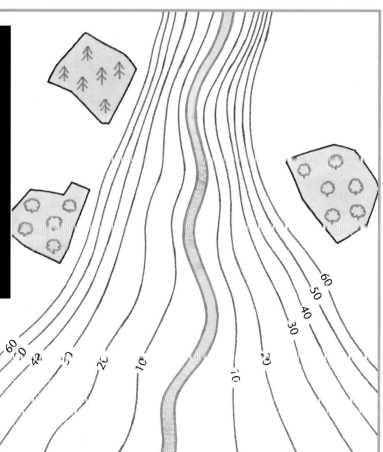

A day by the Derwent

Now let's take a look at the area near the **source** of the River Derwent in the Derbyshire Peak District. At about 80 kilometres long, the River Derwent is the largest river in the Peak District in England.

Counting on contours

The source of the River Derwent is on high ground in Howden Moor. In this **aerial** photograph, we can see the river flowing southwards from its source at the top of the photo. It flows down a **valley** surrounded by **moorland**. If you look at the map on page 19, you can see that this valley is fringed by a lot of brown contour lines drawn very close together. This means that the valley has very steep sides.

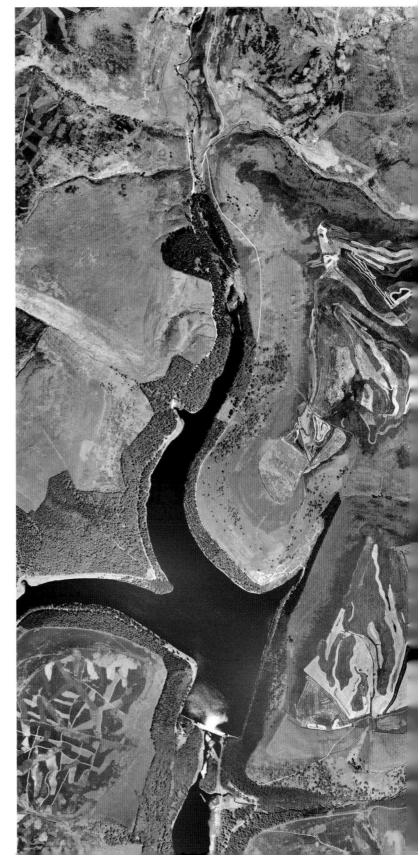

Derwent detectives

Can you see a very large area of water at the southern end of the river in the photo? The label on the map tells us that this is a **reservoir**. It was built in the early 20th century to provide water for people living in nearby cities, such as Derby. We can see from the photograph that the scenery is beautiful. If you look on the map you will see that there are lots of paths and trails. This shows that the area is popular with walkers, cyclists, and tourists.

A smaller river that joins a bigger river is called a **tributary.** Can you see a tributary on this map?
▶ Looking at the numbers on the contour lines, can you tell how high it is at Horse Stone?

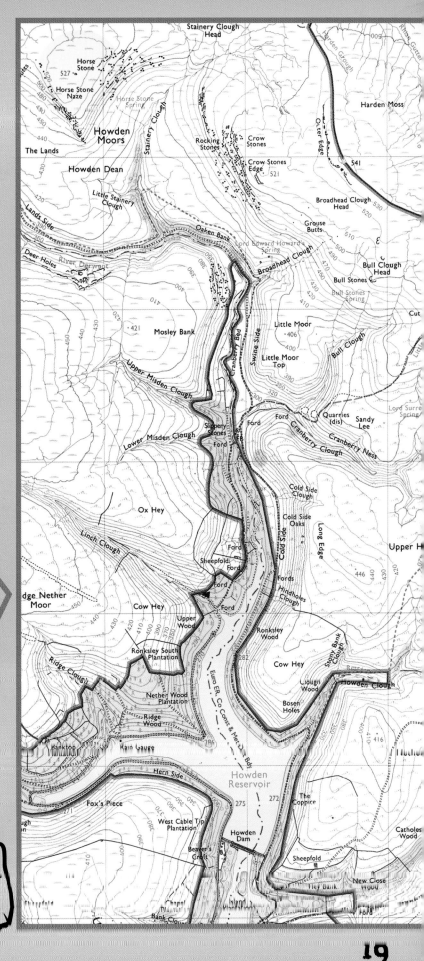

A sense of scale

Have you ever wondered what 'scale' on a map means? Why do different maps have different scales? On a map, features are 'scaled down' in size. This means they are drawn much smaller than they are in real life. Maps can be large scale or small scale. A large-scale map shows a fairly small area of land in a lot of detail. A small-scale map shows a bigger area of land, but with less detail.

The secret of scales

The scale of a map tells you how much bigger an area on the map would be in real life. Scale is given as a number, such as 1:50 000. That means that 1 centimetre on the map is equal to 50,000 centimetres (or 500 metres) in real life. So, if a section of river were 10 centimetres long on a map, it would be 5,000 metres (5 kilometres) long in real life. A map's scale is usually shown on a scale bar. You can see scale bars on the maps opposite.

Grids and scales

Grid squares also help with measuring distance. On an **Ordnance Survey** map each side of a grid square always represents 1 kilometre. By counting grid squares you can work out distances too.

This is the River Wye at Symonds Yat in Herefordshire.

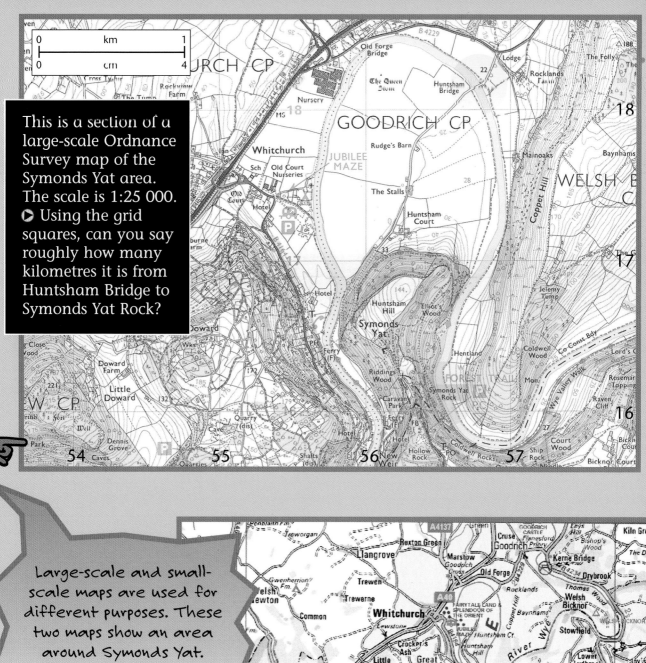

This is a section of a large-scale Ordnance Survey map of the Symonds Yat area. The scale is 1:25 000.
▷ Using the grid squares, can you say roughly how many kilometres it is from Huntsham Bridge to Symonds Yat Rock?

Large-scale and small-scale maps are used for different purposes. These two maps show an area around Symonds Yat.
▶ Which map would you choose if you wanted to go for a walk by the river? Which would be the best map for car drivers?

This road map of the Symonds Yat area is a small-scale map. The scale is 1:100 000.

Rivers of the UK

There are many different kinds of map that show the whole of the UK. Some show where the cities are; some show where the hills and mountains are; others show the areas where rivers are likely to flood in wet weather. The map on this page shows you where some of the main rivers in the UK begin and end.

This map has labels showing the countries in the UK and some of the major cities. This helps you to work out where the rivers are.

The longest river in the UK is the River Severn (354 kilometres). ▶ Which two countries does the Severn flow through?

Shetland Islands

SCOTLAND

R. Tay

N
W E
S

Edinburgh
Glasgow

R. Foyle

Newcastle-upon-Tyne
R. Tyne

N. IRELAND
Belfast

ENGLAND

Manchester
R. Trent

WALES

Birmingham
R. Wye
R. Severn

Cardiff
Bristol
London
R. Avon
R. Thames

0   100 km
0   100 miles

This **aerial** photograph of the British Isles was taken from a **satellite** circling the Earth in space. Mapmakers use photographs like this to make maps of large areas of land, like the one on page 22. The brighter green patches are the low-lying areas that might be more likely to flood in wet weather.

Flooding in UK rivers

Some rivers in the UK are at risk from flooding. Flooding is when a river gets too full and overflows its **banks** on to the surrounding land. Floods are natural events, but they can destroy crops, drown animals in fields, and damage buildings and bridges.

Floods happen when a lot of rain falls into a **river basin** in a fairly short time. Floods usually happen in the middle or lower parts of a river, where the land is flatter. A flood plain is the name for the flat land around a river that can become flooded.

Going global

The Earth is a giant rocky ball that is often represented as a globe. To make a flat paper map of the world, like the one below, mapmakers have to flatten out the globe. Imagine slicing open a football and laying it out flat. Try finding some of the world's rivers on the map below, or on a real globe like the one on the right.

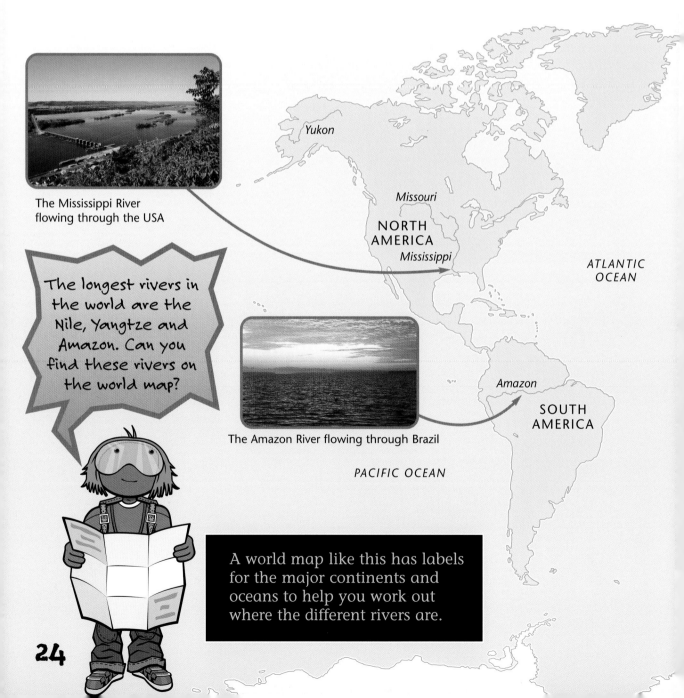

The Mississippi River flowing through the USA

The longest rivers in the world are the Nile, Yangtze and Amazon. Can you find these rivers on the world map?

The Amazon River flowing through Brazil

Yukon

Missouri

NORTH AMERICA

Mississippi

ATLANTIC OCEAN

Amazon

SOUTH AMERICA

PACIFIC OCEAN

A world map like this has labels for the major continents and oceans to help you work out where the different rivers are.

World rivers

The map here shows you some of the world's rivers. These rivers may flow through very different landscapes, but they developed in the same way as UK rivers. Many rivers in the world also share the same problems. Rubbish, oil, chemicals from factories, fertilizers from fields, and **sewage** can cause water **pollution**. Pollution kills wildlife and can make water so dirty that people cannot use it. All around the world, scientists are working to beat the problem of river pollution.

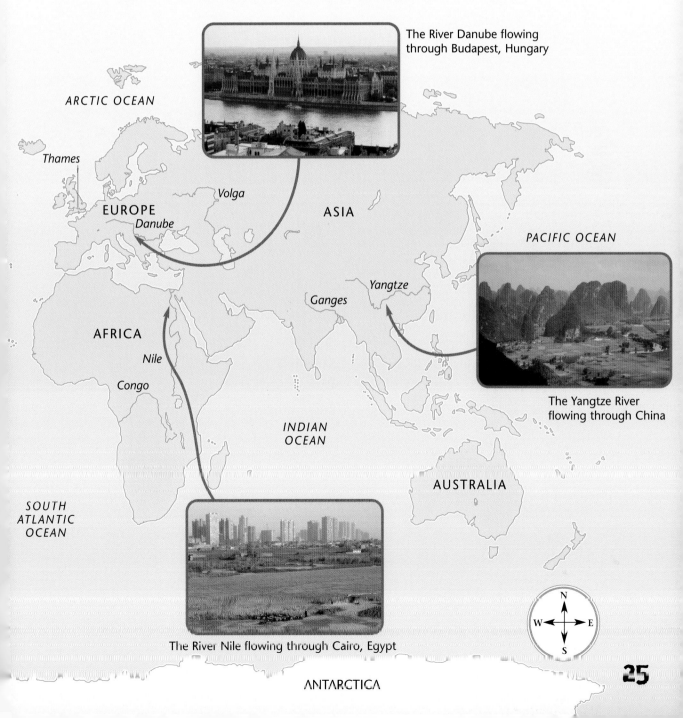

The River Danube flowing through Budapest, Hungary

ARCTIC OCEAN

Thames

Volga

EUROPE

Danube

ASIA

PACIFIC OCEAN

Yangtze

Ganges

AFRICA

Nile

Congo

The Yangtze River flowing through China

INDIAN OCEAN

AUSTRALIA

SOUTH ATLANTIC OCEAN

The River Nile flowing through Cairo, Egypt

ANTARCTICA

Ride a raging river!

Can you paddle a canoe safely through raging white water and down through the gentler **meanders** of a river? Have a go by answering these questions. To find out if you completed your journey successfully, take the first letter of each answer and put them together to make a word.

1 You decide to put your canoe in the water just south of Evil Falls, near the **source** of the river. Soon you are moving very fast downstream, towards Rushing **Rapids**! On the way, you pass a feature on the west **bank** of the river. What is the first letter of its name?

2 Oops! You lose your paddle as you are going over the rapids – and you don't catch up with it until the next **confluence**. What is the first letter of the name of the small **tributary** that joins the main river from the east?

3 You reach the castle, and the river starts to meander. As you go round the first bend, note down the names of the tributaries to the southwest and east of you (in that order). What are the first letters of both names?

4 Which bend in the river will you reach after you have travelled about 2 kilometres south of the castle? Take the first letter of its name.

5 You are hungry, so you stop at grid reference 21, 73 for lunch. What is the first letter of the name of this picnic site?

6 You want to reach the sandy beach without running aground on the mudflats. Which village is on the side of the river that you need to paddle down? What is the first letter of its name?

Now turn to page 29 to see if you made it!

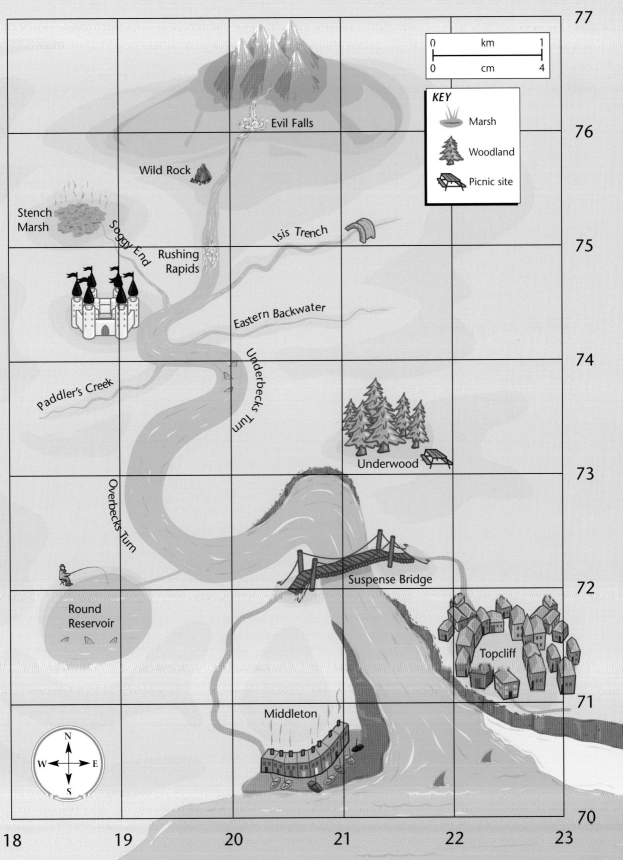

Evil Falls

Wild Rock

Stench
Marsh

Soggy End

Isis Trench

Rushing
Rapids

Eastern Backwater

Underbecks Turn

Paddler's Creek

Underwood

Overbecks Turn

Suspense Bridge

Round
Reservoir

Topcliff

Middleton

km
0   1
0   4
cm

KEY

Marsh

Woodland

Picnic site

N
W   E
S

Quick-stop map skills

What are symbols?

Map symbols are pictures, letters, shapes, lines, or patterns that represent different features, such as rivers and roads. Map keys show what the symbols stand for.

Key

= Bridge	= Marsh

How can I measure distances?

On **Ordnance Survey** maps, each grid square represents 1 kilometre, so you can roughly work out distance by counting grid squares.

What are grid references?

Grid references are numbers that locate a particular square on a map. To give a grid reference, you give the number on the vertical line first and then the number on the horizontal line. ('Along the corridor and up the stairs.')

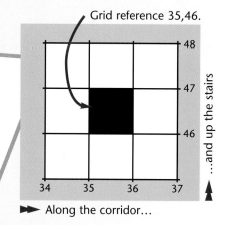

Grid reference 35,46.

...and up the stairs

Along the corridor...

How does scale work?

A map scale tells you how much smaller a feature is on a map than it is in real life. Everything on a map is scaled down in size. On a 1:25 000 scale map, things are 25,000 times smaller than real life.

How are slopes shown on a map?

Maps show slopes by using shaded colours, contour lines, or **gradient** arrows. Gradient arrows look like this >>>. The more arrows, the steeper the slope is. Contour lines join up areas of land that are the same height. When contour lines are close together the slope is steep. When contour lines are spaced out, the land is flatter. Numbers next to, or on the lines tell us the exact height of the land in metres.

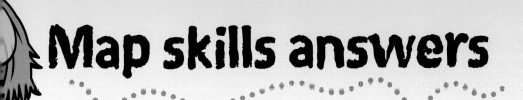

Map skills answers

Page 10/11: The names of the three bridges on the photomap are: 1. Blackfriars Bridge; 2. Waterloo Bridge; 3. Westminster Bridge.

Page 12: Dartmouth is the name of the town at the **mouth** of the River Dart.

Page 13: If you travelled by boat from the **source** of the River Alpha, you would see a footbridge, a picnic site, some slopes, woodland, a road bridge, mud, and some marshy land.

Page14: The grid reference for the **confluence** of the Alpha and Beta Rivers (where they meet) is C,3.

Page 15: The name of the castle in grid 84, 42 is Hanley Castle.
The grid reference for the bridge over the river at Upton upon Severn is 85, 40.
The name of the village at grid reference 87, 39 is Naunton.

Page 19: Horse Stone is 527 metres high.

Page 21: The distance between Huntsham Bridge and Symonds Yat Rock is about 2 kilometres.
The top map (scale 1:25 000) is the best map for walkers because all the footpaths are marked. The map at the bottom of the page (scale 1:100 000) is the best map for drivers. It covers a much larger area of land, and shows all the major roads that link up the towns and villages.

Page 22: The River Severn flows through Wales and England.

Page 26–27: The winning word is WIPEOUT! 1 – W (Wild Rock); 2 – I (Isis Trench); 3 – P (Paddler's Creek) and E (Eastern Backwater); 4 – O (Overbecks Turn); 5 – U (Underwood); 6 – T (Topcliff).

Glossary

aerial overhead, from the sky

banks sides of a river or stream between which the water usually flows

channel the route through which a river flows between its banks

confluence place where two rivers or streams join together

deposited dropped

erosion when rocks or land are worn away by wind, water, ice, or by people

estuary part of a river where it widens and meets the sea

evaporate when water turns from a liquid into a vapour

gradient steepness of a slope

meander large bend in the course of a river

moorland high, exposed area of land

mouth end of a river, where it flows into the sea or a lake

Ordnance Survey map-making organization that makes maps that cover the whole of the UK

permanent features things that are always in the same place in a landscape, such as bridges or roads

pollution when water, air, or soil are made dirty or poisonous by people's waste

rapids when a river flows very quickly and swirls around over rocks

reservoir lake formed by damming a river to store water that can be piped to settlements

river basin area of land from which all the water drains into a particular river. Also called a catchment area.

riverbed bottom of the river

satellite scientific object that orbits the Earth in space and sends out TV signals or takes photographs

sediment small bits of soil or rock that are transported by water and then deposited on the river bed or the banks

sewage human bodily waste carried away from homes and other buildings in drainage pipes

source beginning of a stream or river

spring place where water comes up from under the ground to form a stream

tributary stream or river that flows into bigger stream, river or a lake

valley land shaped like a 'v', with sloping sides and often with a river flowing along the bottom

waterfall point where a river suddenly drops over a ledge of rock. Waterfalls form where a layer of hard rock sits above softer rock. The river wears away the soft rock creating a ledge.

Find out more

Books

Wild Habitats: Rivers and Waterways, Louise and Richard Spilsbury (Heinemann Library, 2004)

Great Rivers of Britain and Ireland (Great Rivers), Michael Pollard (Evans Brothers, 2002)

Philip's Junior Atlas (4th edn), (Heinemann, Rigby, Ginn, 2003)

Websites

You can play games, get homework help and learn more about using maps on the Ordnance Survey Mapzone site:
www.ordnancesurvey.co.uk/mapzone

The Environment Agency has information about waters and rivers in the UK and factsheets and advice about flooding:
www.environment-agency.gov.uk/fun

Join Fergal the Frog for a trip down the River Trent to see lots of aerial photos of the river area, and some maps too:
www.sln.org.uk/trentweb

Check out the geography section on the Heinemann Explore website to find out even more about maps!
www.heinemannexplore.co.uk

Have fun with maps in the future – you should never get lost again!

Index